dog food

concept by Judith Adler

photographs by Paul Coughlin

RODALE

To all the dogs who have fed my soul,

especially my beloved Pele, for the feast of love you

always served up with a wag and a smile.—J.A.

•

To Jerry, Connie, Sabina, Nuna, and Aura. —P.C.

Printed in China

Rodale Inc. makes every effort to use acid-free ∞, recycled paper ♺.

Book design by Maggie Hinders

Library of Congress Cataloging-in-Publication Data

Adler, Judith.
    Dog food / concept by Judith Adler ; photographs by Paul Coughlin.
        p.   cm.
    ISBN 1–59486–105–6 hardcover
    1. Dogs—Pictorial works.   2. Dogs—Food—Pictorial works.   3. Photography of dogs.   4. Quotations, English.   I. Coughlin, Paul.   II. Title.
    SF430.A39   2004
    636.7'0022'2—dc22   2004014397

Distributed to the trade by Holtzbrinck Publishers

2 4 6 8 10 9 7 5 3 1 hardcover

Acknowledgments

To our wise agent Susan Golomb, thank you for your guidance, inspiration, and support. To our gifted editor Margot Schupf, many thanks for another vision realized under your wise, patient, ever-more Zen stewardship. Many thanks to Sara Sellar for your mindfulness and presence; your support and kindness are greatly appreciated. To Patricia Field, thank you for your guiding hand and artistic impeccability (and the pancakes!). To Jennifer Reich, thank you for your attention to detail. To Maggie Hinders, the elegant designer whose brilliant design has graced all of our books, our gratitude for your light, mindfulness, whimsy, and charm that shines through on every page! It is truly a gift to create these gifts with you. A gracious thank you to Amira Pierce, Kim Goldstein, and John Moses for your myriad talents. For their technical support, we thank Josh Weiss, David Rajwan, Marti Andersen, Shalom Ben-Yosef, Zeke Rosenson, Josh Snow, Ruby Cabrera, and Heather Brandon. For their photographic assistance, we thank Ogie Sevilla, Rhomy Del Rosario, and Alan Tang.

Additional thanks go to The Washington Square Dog Run Association, especially Pat, and the Washington Square Animal Hospital, for their helpfulness on this project, especially Dr. Ann Lucas, Dr. Kristin Kutscher, Joan Debellis, Fredi Grieshaber, Addie West, and Pat Fusco. Thank you also to Gina Ruiz at Chumley's for giving us the secret password to shoot in your historic restaurant.

Grateful acknowledgments go to Robert and Andrea Perkel, Donald Williams, Jane and Robert Gordon (with fond memories of Cody), as well as to Jane Perkel and one of the sweetest dog-lovers ever, Monae Wright.

To all our soul friends and family whose love has fed our spirits along the way, thank you for offering up food for thought when we were hungry for ideas, spiritual nourishment when our souls' bellies were rumbling, and nutritious support when we were dragging our tails. You each contributed just the right ingredient to the recipe of our success.

Introduction

A dog desires affection more than dinner. Well, almost.

—CHARLOTTE GRAY

"Did anyone feed the dog?" is a refrain heard the world over, in countless languages. Yet, metaphorically speaking, no one ever has to ask if the dog has fed us. In their panting, barking, yipping mother tongue, the non-verbal language of love, dogs feed our spirits constantly. From that "oh boy, oh boy, you're home, you're home!!!!" dance they greet us with when we come home dog-tired from work, to that turbo charged wag of gratitude when we toss them bones, the unconditional love dogs offer us is clearly food for our souls.

Sure we might share an occasional nacho with them, but a chip or two is no match for the whole enchilada. Your beagle might not be keen on giving you the bone from his mouth, but he'll give you the smile off his face. Simply put, dogs simply love us. They ask for so very little, and they give so very much.

Dogs serve us so devotedly that if they could save us the trouble and make their own dinners, they probably would. Alas, the lack of opposable thumbs makes opening their own Alpo

> Ask not what you can do for your country. Ask what's for lunch.
>
> —ORSON WELLES

impossible and hunting and gathering would be out of place in the suburbs, hence dogs' total dependence on us. Yet it's a happy dependence. Even for providing a plain bowl of kibble, we are treated to displays of gratitude humans would reserve for winning the lottery. For most dogs, dinnertime is the main event.

Maybe that's why even if your dog just finished eating a bowl of food, she'll still look up at you with *that* look. You know the look all too well. It's that pitiful gaze into your soul with those hungry—no, *starving*—eyes. All this begging begs the question, if dogs are getting plenty to eat, why such pleading? We can look to their ancestors for clues. In the wild, wolves never know where their next meal is coming from, so when opportunity presents itself they gorge themselves. Domestic canines haven't lost this opportunistic trait. They eat as much, as often, as possible. Their physiological makeup helps, too. Even a medium-size dog's stomach will stretch to hold more than a gallon of food.

So with all this constant hunger, but without the means to get food on their own, our dogs are completely dependent on us to feed them. Just how do they get us to do that? The expression "puppy dog eyes" didn't come from nowhere! It seems every dog is born with them, as well as the switch to turn them on at will, especially when there's a shot at your sandwich. Some dogs, take Jack Russell terriers for instance, actually beg with their whole bodies. These brilliant beggars maintain perfectly poised posture that's so focused an Olympic athlete would envy their concentration.

Other dogs are simply masters of opportunity. Dogs station themselves strategically under tables, vigilantly scoping their territories, where anything and everything that falls is fair game. It's a dog's version of manna from heaven. If dogs said prayers, "God, please let that pot roast take a tumble" would probably be first on their list.

Here's another familiar canine plot for food: Dogs look longingly at the food, then stare at you for a moment, then look back at the food, then back at you again (a little more intensely this time), and then quickly back to the food. It is as if they're trying Kreskin mind-control tactics. "You *want* to feed me, you *will* feed me, you *must* feed me . . . "

Then there's the "eat first, ask questions later" club. These dogs are astonishingly adept at catching treats in their mouths. Once in a while they regret the decision, but not very often. Fetching a Frisbee might be fun, but popcorn, peanuts, heck, pretty much anything to eat, is far better.

Dogs use another age-old tradition to sweet-talk us into giving them food: licking. Wait, isn't that simply affection? Perhaps, but then again it might just be a throwback to innate canine nature. Conventional wisdom holds that subordinates lick alpha canines as a sign of respect. Modern mutts, entreating us to give them

> Our lives are not in the lap of the gods, but in the lap of our cooks.
>
> —LIN YUTANG

more treats, know that lots of humans find this licking business charming, reading it as a sign of affection rather than a ploy for more food. They make us feel like top dog, which with a little luck will help them get top-quality food.

> **Happy are those with a delicate palate and a cast-iron throat.**
>
> —GRIMOD DE LA REYNIÈRE

Another doggie secret is stealthiness. These dogs' hunting instincts certainly haven't been lost. But today instead of stalking small animals, they stalk leftovers. Success, real success, is scoring a precious tidbit off your plate, *now*. Other dogs are a bit less refined about getting food from their people. These pooches are bulldogs in Chinese restaurants when it comes to the prospect of a bite of your egg roll or, dare they dream, a sparerib bone. Look away for a second, and they'll snatch it!

With all this talk lately of returning to the traditional family dinner, maybe we could learn from the four-leggeds under the four legs of the table. Dogs are social creatures, often waiting to eat until their people friends return home, even if the bowl has been full all day. Dogs know instinctively that food and companionship is a great combination. That's why they'll follow you anywhere to get some.

As the old saw goes, "Every dog has his day!" Here's hoping this book will inspire you to see the love, devotion, compassion, and doggone charm in your favorite dogs to make today *their* day. All it takes is some love—although a tiny bite of your pastrami sandwich or a little nibble of that pork chop would be nice, too.

My dog is worried about the economy

because Alpo is up to 99 cents a can.

That's almost $7.00 in dog money.

—JOE WEINSTEIN

THE
diner IS EVERYBODY'S
kitchen.

—RICHARD GUTMAN

Life is a combination
of magic and pasta.

—FEDERICO FELLINI

The second day of a diet

is always easier than the first.

By the second day **you're off it.**

—JACKIE GLEASON

What do snowmen eat for breakfast?

S
N   O
W   F   L
A
K
E
S.

—ANONYMOUS

The universe is full of *magical things,*

PATIENTLY WAITING

for our *wits* to grow sharper.

—PHILL POTTS

It's not the size of the

dog in the fight,

it's the size of the

fight in the dog.

—MARK TWAIN

Yesterday I was **a dog.**

Today I'm **a dog.**

Tomorrow I'll probably still be **a dog.**

There's so little hope for advancement.

—SNOOPY

Life expectancy would grow by leaps and bounds if green vegetables smelled as good as bacon.

—DOUG LARSON

I'm in shape. Round's a shape.

—ANONYMOUS

Coffee led GREEK CIVILIZATION to reach

its heights of art and philosophy.

—JIM TRAPP

Don't eat until you're **full;**

eat until you're ti**red!**

—HAWAIIAN SAYING

I don't
eat anything that
a dog won't eat. Like
sushi. Ever see a dog eat
sushi? He just sniffs it and
says, "I don't think so."
And this is an animal
that sniffs fire
hydrants.

—BILLIAM CORONEL

Watermelon, it's a good fruit.

You eat,

you drink,

you wash your face.

—ENRICO CARUSO

Happiness
Happiness
Happiness
Happiness
Happiness

never decreases by being shared.

—BUDDHA

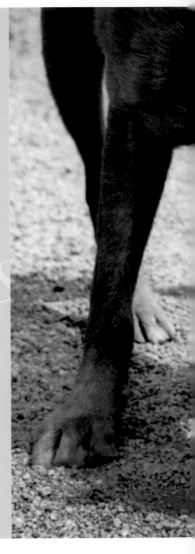

The golden rule

when reading the menu is

if you can not *pronounce* it,

you can not *afford* it.

—FRANK MUIR

I finally managed to teach my dog to beg.

Last night he came home with 15 bucks.

—ANONYMOUS

Some say the glass is **half empty,**

some say the glass is **half full,**

I say,

"Are you going to drink that?"

—LISA CLAYMEN

Fools rush in where *angels* fear to tread.

—ALEXANDER POPE

No animal should ever jump up

on the dining-room furniture

unless absolutely certain

that he can hold his own in the conversation.

—FRAN LEBOWITZ

In a restaurant, *choose* *a* **table** *near a* waiter.

—JEWISH PROVERB

You may have a **dog**

that won't sit up, roll over, or even cook breakfast,

not because **she's too stupid to learn how,**

but because **she's too *smart* to bother.**

—RICK HOROWITZ

It's a

DOG
EAT
DOG
world,

and I'm running

out of napkins.

—ANONYMOUS

There is no small **pleasure** in sweet water.

—OVID

If you are what you eat,

I'm fast, cheap, and easy.

—ANONYMOUS

You cannot find here

any piece of meat

that is not the **BEST.**

—ZEN KOAN

It's important to watch what you eat.

Otherwise, how are you

going to get it into your mouth?

—MATT DIAMOND

FOOD
is our common ground, a universal experience.

—JAMES BEARD

If at first you don't succeed, **ORDER PIZZA.**

—ANONYMOUS

If you think

dogs can't count,

try putting three

dog biscuits

in your pocket

and then giving

Fido only two

of them.

—PHIL PASTORET

Small cheer and great **welcome** makes a *merry feast.*

—WILLIAM SHAKESPEARE

Dogs have given us their absolute all.

We are the center of their universe.

We are the focus of their love and faith and trust.

They serve us in return for scraps.

It is without a doubt the best deal man has ever made.

—ROGER CARAS

When we lose, I eat.

When we win, I eat.

I also eat when we're rained out.

—TOMMY LASORDA

I DIDN'T STRUGGLE TO THE top

of the

food chain

to be a vegetarian.

—ANONYMOUS

Smell is a potent wizard that transports us across thousands

—HELEN KELLER

of miles and all the years we have lived.

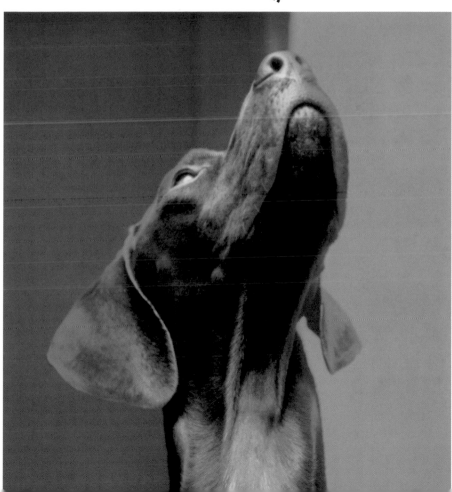

RECIPE:

A series of step-by-step instructions

for preparing ingredients you forgot to buy,

in utensils you don't own,

to make a dish the **dog** wouldn't eat.

—ANONYMOUS

He has been eating things
I know he doesn't like,
just to get even . . . things like
socks and mittens and paper napkins,
which, of course, are delicious.

—JEAN KERR

The **dog** wags his tail,

not for you,

but for your **bread.**

—PORTUGUESE PROVERB

When you have only

two pennies

left in the world,

buy a loaf of bread with one,

and a *lily* with the other.

—CHINESE PROVERB

Time is

an illusion.

Lunchtime

doubly so.

—DOUGLAS ADAMS

A well-trained dog will make no attempt to share your lunch. He will just make you feel so guilty that you cannot enjoy it.

—HELEN THOMSON

I was raised by a pack of **wild**

corn dogs.

—ANONYMOUS

It has become appallingly obvious

that our **TECHNOLOGY**

has exceeded our *humanity.*

—ALBERT EINSTEIN

It's nice to eat a good hunk of **beef,**

but you want a *light dessert,* too.

—ARTHUR FIEDLER

A

smiling

face

is

half

the

meal.

—LATVIAN PROVERB

People who count their chickens

before they are hatched act very wisely

because afterwards

chickens

run about

so *absurdly*

that it is impossible to count them ACCURATELY.

—OSCAR WILDE

Measure the **girth**

of the chef

and you can rate his restaurant.

—FRENCH SAYING

If this is coffee, please bring me tea;

if this is tea, please bring me coffee.

—ABRAHAM LINCOLN

You don't sew with a fork, so I see no reason to eat with knitting needles.

—MISS PIGGY

Get a good idea and stay with it.

DOG it and work at it until it's done right.

—WALT DISNEY

 *The time* goes to every dog

when it ceases to care for people merely for biscuits or bones

or even caresses and walks outdoors.

When a dog really loves, it prefers the person who gives it nothing.

—FRANCES P. COBBE

Photo Credits

FRONT COVER: Lola Calway (Jack Russell terrier); **PAGE 2:** Annie Girl (beagle) with food bowl; **PAGE 6:** Annabelle and Breeda O'Sullivan (Jack Russell terriers) eating ice cream; **PAGE 13:** Brock (Jack Russell terrier) at the Empire Diner, New York; **PAGE 14:** Annie AKA "Orion's Andromeda" (West Highland terrier) with pasta; **PAGE 17:** Zico (Brazilian Fila) profile; **PAGE 18:** C.J. (Border collie) in snow; **PAGE 21:** Zoë Tsunami Siegler (Australian shepherd) with can opener; **PAGE 22:** Jack Mayhew (miniature pinscher) with bone; **PAGE 25:** Gus Sheehy (Doberman) at the Gansevoort Market; **PAGE 26:** Scout "the Dog" Gruhn with bacon; **PAGE 29:** Bulldog puppy; **PAGE 30:** Mo (Rottweiler) with cup; **PAGE 32:** Grand Pyrenees on bench; **PAGE 35:** Ludwig at fire hydrant; **PAGE 36:** Penelope "Penny" Dennis (boxer) with watermelon; **PAGE 39:** Bean with friend at water bowl; **PAGE 40:** Skylos (American bulldog) with menu at Chumleys; **PAGE 43:** Charley Barnett begging; **PAGE 44:** Katie Scarlett O'Kern (toy poodle) with wine glass; **PAGE 46:** Maxine Kern, (Yorkshire terrier) in treat jar; **PAGE 49:** Sadie Goldstein (Portuguese water dog) in bowl; **PAGE 50:** Zander (weimaraner) at café; **PAGE 53:** Mr. Socks Cericola (cockapoo) with pancakes; **PAGE 54:** Lulu (dachshund) as a hot dog; **PAGE 56:** Paxil (cairn terrier) drinking water; **PAGE 58:** Afghan "Paws For a Cause" Dog Walk, New York; **PAGE 60:** Spartacus (poodle) at the Alleva Dairy, Little Italy, New York; **PAGE 63:** Sammie (yellow Lab) with biscuit; **PAGE 64:** "K2" (Jack Russell terrier) with Karachi, Inner Circle Farm, Patterson, New York; **PAGE 67:** Bungie Perkel (Shiba Inu) with pizza; **PAGE 68:** Deke with Gary; **PAGE 71:** Maverick at Chumbley's, New York; **PAGE 73:** Bounder (golden retriever) with doggie bag; **PAGE 74:** Wet French bulldog, Washington Square Dog Run; **PAGE 77:** Snowball Pugliese with saddlebag; **PAGE 79:** Maverick Ruiz sniffing air; **PAGE 81:** Duke (basset hound) in chef's hat; **PAGE 83:** Reese Meisel (dachshund) with rawhide; **PAGE 84:** Maisie (Airedale terrier) at Vesuvio Bakery; **PAGE 87:** Kara Golomb-Martin at flower market; **PAGE 88:** Reflection Greenwich Village; **PAGE 91:** Mushy (Boston terrier); **PAGE 92:** Haggis (cairn terrier) with corn; **PAGE 95:** Maggie (bulldog) and Annie (beagle) as dishwashers; **PAGE 96:** Lucy Ansley Ungar (English cocker spaniel) with Richard of Empire Purveyors; **PAGE 99:** Parisian poodle; **PAGE 100:** Igor (Dalmatian) with chicken; **PAGE 103:** Maggie (bulldog) at Joe's Pizza; **PAGE 104:** Scrappy (Chihuahua) in coffee pot; **PAGE 107:** Belly Levine (Shih Tzu) with chopsticks; **PAGE 108:** "K2" (Jack Russell terrier) with bone; **PAGE 110:** Spaniel Embrace, Washington Square Dog Run.

Photographs are by Paul Coughlin with the exception of pages 21, 36, and 99, which are by Judith Adler.